Dear Jane

It's NOT Me ...

Saying Goodbye
to Self-Criticism
and Hello to
Self-Love,
Confidence
and Courage

LORI GENTLES

Dear Jane – It's NOT Me . . .

Copyright © 2023 Lori Gentles

Cover illustration by Tara Thelen
Design by Deborah Perdue, Illumination Grapics
Stock art courtesy of shutterstock.com and depositphotos.com

Paperback ISBN: 979-8-9887611-0-5

Dedication

In words that echo Snoop Dogg,

I want to thank me for having the courage
to push forward against all odds, to walk in my rhythm
and to care not what others think of me.

I also dedicate this book to those who dare to do
the same . . .

Contents

Acknowledgment

· ·

Thanks to all the good and positive people in my life. You affirm that the universe is on my side. I would be remiss if I didn't also give thanks for negative forces that have passed through my life. Your presence brought discomfort and motivated me to action. I am grateful because "All things are working together for my good."

Definition

· ·

Jane/jān/

Noun

"A person, place, thing or concept, or a person who causes,
produces or represents
just additional negative energy."
—Lori Gentles

Dear Jane Letter

A letter written to end a relationship that is no longer working for you. Sometimes such a letter is written to a romantic
partner, as in the infamous Dear John letters. In this case,
Jane is gender neutral and represents the relationship you
have with your job, friends, boss, school, church, family, and,
most important, the negative side of you that is no longer
working for you. Jane is Just Additional Negative Energy that
you don't need—Amen?

Introduction

Psst! Listen up. This matter concerns you. This entire book is all about you and the serious problem you probably didn't even know you have. Your condition might be so severe that you are in grave danger, if you don't take action to address and reverse the problem. This condition is rarely properly diagnosed.

Millions of people suffer from the condition year after year. It typically goes unnoticed and untreated for decades. People learn to live with it, I *guess*. Sadly, some people even go to their graves with this condition, having been cheated out of the fullness of health and well-being they could have had. Unlike cancer that eats away at your body, this condition eats away at your body, mind and soul. Some people become crippled, paralyzed, a prisoner in their own bodies.

There is no medicine you can take to alleviate the condition. There is no radiation or chemical treatments you can endure to zap away the condition. There is no surgery you can have to fix or remove what is ailing you. Don't bother with physical therapy or strength training. It won't work for this condition. Any human-made, external treatment, process or procedure cannot cure it.

This condition is so severe, that the only way you can cure it is by accessing a unique, personalized and specialized treatment plan that is curated just for you. Like an episode from the 1959 television series, *The Twilight Zone*, this mysterious and lingering condition is you and the cure is you. Now that I have your attention, please read on.

This book is about the struggle we have listening, heeding, succumbing to and embracing the negative voice of others that dampens our spirits and limits our beliefs. It is also about the voice that germinates from within us and resounds loudly in our own head. The voice is super loud, like golden cymbals in a marching band vigorously banged together unexpectedly.

The voice is sometimes subtle, quiet but powerful, driving us to behave like zombies—doing things and behaving in ways we wouldn't if we were fully awake. The voice is always obnoxious and always present, nagging at us when we dare to be great. The voice is super sneaky, sly like a fox, slithering through our minds like a serpent, constantly whispering in our mind's consciousness, planting seeds of doubt, untruths and promises that lead to our demise.

Do you remember the Bible story in Genesis when the serpent convinced Eve to eat the forbidden fruit with the promise that she would gain all wisdom? If you continue to read the story, you know the outcome was not good for Adam or Eve. Such will be your outcome if you stay on this path.

The voice is bold and audacious, telling us what we can and cannot do, telling us what we should or shouldn't do. It tells us we are not good enough, smart enough, pretty or handsome enough. It tells us that we are not capable, that we are just average, that we will never achieve nor do we deserve anything greater than what we have this moment.

You know that there are many critics able and willing to keep you stuck in your place by feeding you limiting words and thoughts. That's a given. However, before you start to identify, name and blame others for their criticism of you . . . before you start to cast stones . . . first look in the mirror.

Mirror, mirror, on the wall, am I the worst critic of all? Now seriously, are you your worst critic? You've heard the saying that the real enemy is within you. Take a long look at yourself. Is it true? Are you your biggest obstacle? Are you your supreme dream killer? With friends like you, you don't need a Jane. You are Jane and you draw other Janes to you. Jane, in its many forms is a close and most wicked companion. Jane manifested as a person, place or thing is Just Additional Negative Energy impacting and influencing you in unproductive and harmful ways.

According to the science of quantum physics, everything is energy. As humans we have vibrational energy that is either positive or negative. I read a LinkedIn article that said your thoughts, the company you keep, the music you listen to, what you watch, your environment, what you speak and your level of gratitude causes your vibrational energy to be either positive or negative. That is why saying goodbye to Jane is a matter of human well-being.

Not all connections are good. Some breakups are necessary. Sometimes we need to disconnect from relationships quickly and in a hurry. Some breakups are a matter of life or death—figuratively and literally. Relationships that bring prolonged stress, anxiety and heartache, that kill your spirit, your soul and your essence or cause you to want to harm yourself or others, must end as soon as possible.

This concept is difficult for many people because endings can be sad. The end of an era, the end of youth, the end of summer and the end of football season all bring a certain level of sadness with the recognition that this time has passed forever. Fortunately, there is another option that creates a different, healthier emotion. It's called release.

Release as an action is to deliberately choose to return to a resting place by removing pressure. It's like forgiveness. When you actively decide to forgive someone for a wrong, you relieve the pressure from you. It's not about granting relief to the offender. Deciding to release is still scary but once you decide to let go of what you've known for so long, what you've come to tolerate and accept as normal, you will feel more optimistic about the future instead of nostalgic about the past.

I've had to release a lot of bad connections in my past and I assume there will be others I will have to release as long as I'm alive. It is the cycle of life. It is unrealistic to think that you will never experience unpleasantness again.

Seasons come and seasons go but once you realize, like in the *Game of Thrones*, that "winter is coming," you can prepare and not get frostbitten.

Identify your Jane (it might be the person staring back at you in the mirror), then repeat after me.

"Dear Jane, I'm leaving you. Goodbye."

Chapter 1:

· ·

Release—It's Over!
Bye-Bye, Jane

Release/rə'lēs/
Verb

"Allow or enable to escape from confinement; set free."
—*Verve Basket*

Yep. You heard me correctly. I am breaking up
with you. Our decades-long relationship is finally over. Why
did it take me this long? Over the years I've come to realize
that I've been blaming and criticizing myself for everything,
excusing you, giving you a pass, trying to soothe you, all at my
expense. I thought I was being good, supportive, loving, rising
above it all and being the bigger better person. Truth be told,
I was weak and I gave my power away.

I suffered from low self-esteem. I esteemed you higher than
myself. And with every unwarranted apology, "I'm sorry . . ."
With every doing "extra" to make you see that I'm worthy, valued, a contributor, important, I would shrink lower and lower.
Any semblance of confidence that I tried to muster continued
to wane. Was that your plan, to tear me down so that you could
stand? Was your plan to minimize me so that you could be max-
imized or to discredit me so that you could take all the credit?
To ridicule, shame and belittle me so that I would give up, give
in, sit down, do as I'm told, keep silent and hide my brilliance?

Hah! You silly rabbit. Tricks are for kids. I'm all grown up
now in age and wisdom. So no more Jane. Call it age, call it I
just don't give a damn, call it sick and tired of being tired and
abused. I don't really care because after all these years, I have
finally seen the light and guess what? It's not me . . . it's you.

I'm determined to break free once and for all. Free from
guilt and shame. Free from playing the small game. You
know the game that's kind of like hide-and-go-seek. I hide

and try to become invisible. It works because I'm never found. No one is really trying to find me until of course they need me to serve their needs.

The game is one-sided. Because I'm never found, I never get to seek. As a result I never find what I need. How fair is that? Perhaps these games and tricks are acceptable, tolerable and even fun as children. But as an adult—ain't nobody got time for all that.

I plan to be free from feeling less than but pretending to be more than. Free from my identity crisis—always asking who am I?—then giving a fake answer and doing fake things to support the fake image. When you don't know who you are, fakeness abounds; it's everywhere. You see it on social media.

People taking and posting a thousand pictures of themselves in sexy poses pretending to be living their best life. These people only highlight a superficial layer of what they want you to see. It's a desperate attempt to convince themselves that they are OK. "Look at me! I'm great. I have it all together. I'm successful. Don't you see how happy I am? Don't you see all of my stuff?" Now accept me please.

Sadly, many people see this façade and start to feel bad or worse about themselves because "they don't have it together" like the person in the picture. What they fail to realize is that many of those people are hiding and disguising their low self-esteem and lack of confidence behind "stuff" that they probably can't afford and don't need. Stuff that no one cares about, like them sipping on a Swiss mocha latte at the upscale café. Stuff, like their purse/shoe/tie/car collection.

Don't get me wrong, it's a blessing to have stuff. The question is are you hiding behind stuff? Are you hiding your feelings of inadequacy, deficiency, loneliness, sadness, depression and worse yet, emptiness? Are you trying to shine a light in the darkness with bling this and bling that instead of letting your inner light shine?

Here's a good one—are you using your stuff to gain acceptance and validation from people who are not worthy of your attention, who you don't even know and who wouldn't come to your funeral if you died today? Are you trapped in the faulty belief system, whose underlying yet faulty belief is that you're not enough but others and everything else are?

If you lost everything today, would you survive or be on the brink of suicide? Sadly, we know those people whose identities and self-esteem are tied to material things (a job, a title, a home, other possessions). When those things are taken away (for example, bad investments, organizational change/layoff, natural disaster, divorce), they go into a deep depression and some actually kill themselves.

"Hi, my name is Lori, and I am a recovering shopaholic."
Everyone say, "Hi, Lori."

I've been sober now for decades, having done the work to fill my need for approval with love, peace and goodness instead of clothes, and more clothes and for heaven's sake more clothes. I was in disguise, an imposter. A little black girl, growing up in a mostly Mexican and Black neighborhood of modest means, I thought the outer appearance would make me whole, better, accepted and make me appear to have greater means than I had. Nice clothes, shoes and all the fix-ins would make people think I had it all together.

It worked for a while. "Faking it 'til you make it" is a real thing until it's not. Heck, I even fooled myself temporarily until I was forced to face the truth about me and then make a change. There comes a time in life where the rubber meets the road. Where fake you meets real you.

This is eerie and reminiscent of the science fiction television series, *The Twilight Zone*, that I used to love to watch. Each episode highlighted essential truths about humanity. The characters had to face their truth and the consequence of their actions. Each episode was a full-on encounter with the inner self. You didn't know you had a double who is at war with you, did you? The real you at some point will have to show up confidently and competently or be found to be a fraud.

I can recall many instances when my outer display of confidence did not match my inner feelings of inadequacy. You've been there, I'm sure. Thank goodness for Google and Siri. Now when I'm in a situation where I don't know something, I can call on my lifeline. I can quickly research what I don't know and respond as if I knew all along. Whew. This beats pretending that I understand the reference in a conversation or business meeting when I have no clue. But seriously, these days if I don't know something, I confidently just admit it. No sense in trying to fool anyone. Pretending perpetuates lack of confidence.

I remember being in my twenties and early in my human resources career. Google and Siri did not exist then. *Side note: I'm really not as ancient as it sounds*. New technologies are created rapidly and what's not present today is all of a sudden present tomorrow. I was ambitious and worked harder and smarter than others, filling gaps and doing tasks that needed to be done. I did work that no one else wanted to do or felt empowered to do. *Side note: I did this without complaint, as I was eager to learn everything I could and leverage it for something bigger.*

Today it seems that most people are poverty/scarcity oriented and won't do one thing extra if they are not paid for it. This is a losing mentality. Greediness in general but especially in the workplace bothers me—but that's a topic for another book. My approach landed me in positions of considerable responsibility for someone my age, being in meetings with CEOs and heads of departments, attorneys, discussing a personnel related matter in or approaching litigation.

Even though I was smart, hardworking, and used my interpersonal communications degree flawlessly to ensure that the first impression of me was impressive, there were times when the "old" people (when you are twenty-one, someone thirty-five is old—someone fifty is ancient), would ask for my opinion on something they had just said using words and sophisticated phraseology and references that I just didn't know.

Too shy, embarrassed and lacking courage and confidence to simply say, "I'm not sure I understand," I'd fake it, redirect or ramble and then feel utterly stupid for hours, days, weeks after. I would beat myself up, playing the scenario over and over again. How could I be so dumb? Why didn't I know this or that (as if I can know every question and point of reference of all time)?

It was an unrealistic expectation I placed on myself. It was an invisible straitjacket that served to immobilize and restrain me. Jane, the pesky and ubiquitous "friend," wouldn't leave me alone.

Self-Reflection Journal Entry
Your Inner Jane

☆ What mistakes or decisions have you made that you still ruminate over to this day?

_____

_____

_____

☆ Are you reliving, retraumatizing and beating your-self up for the mistake?

_____

_____

_____

☆ What ways can you stop retraumatizing yourself?

_____

_____

_____

Did you know that your brain doesn't distinguish between a real situation and an imagined one? Doctors say that your brain produces stress hormones (for example, adrenalin and cortisol) when you remember something that has happened in the past or when you imagine a situation.

Jane and your brain are bullies, always criticizing, poking and provoking. If you don't care about yourself, Jane certainly won't. Jane can sniff you out a mile away and will always harass you until you kick her/him/them/it to the curb. By the way, bullies are only bullies until you stand up to them and give them a dose of their own medicine. A swift punch in the face will do the trick. I'm not advocating violence, of course . . . but if you don't take action, bullies become more empowered and more taunting.

☆ What is your inner Jane telling you now?

_____

_____

_____

☆ What is Jane's motivation? Is the message uplifting you or tearing you down?

_____

_____

_____

☆ What can you do to silence Jane?

_____

_____

_____

☆ What will you do when Jane returns?

_____

_____

_____

Jane, oh Jane, you are insane. Jane, you must refrain from getting in my brain. I see you clearly for who and what you are—a bully, a hater, a master manipulator. You want to keep me down, approaching life with a frown. I'm on to you and I know that you are a clown. Party over, Bozo. Your time is up. I'm rising, I'm standing, walking boldly toward my goals, and where I'm going you simply cannot go.

In 1947, years before she met John F. Kennedy, seventeen-year-old Jacqueline Lee Bouvier sent her twenty-one-year-old Harvard boyfriend this Dear John (Jane) letter.

"I've always thought of being in love as being willing to do anything for the other person—starve to buy them bread and not mind living in Siberia with them—and I've always thought that every minute away from them would be hell—so looking at it that [way] I guess I'm not in love with you."

Chapter 2:

Regroup—
What Did I Just Do?

Regroup/rē'groop
Verb

"To stop for a short time and prepare yourself before you continue doing something that is difficult: to stop and think, reorganize, etc., before continuing."
—*The Britannica Dictionary*

Regroup

Congratulations! You succeeded in the first test of courage. It takes courage to overcome your fear and take action even though you are fearful of the outcome. Courage is not the absence of fear but it is facing the fear, embracing it and rising above it. When you chose to release—you may, for a split second, have asked, "What did I just do?" That seed of doubt is a test, a test of your will, your clarity and your confidence.

Sure, we've acknowledged that breaking up is hard to do. Even if the relationship is unhealthy, deciding to move on can be scary. The thought of the unknown keeps us paralyzed. That's one reason why so many people choose to stay in dysfunction. Whether you're in a toxic work environment, bad marriage, abusive one-sided friendship or fraudulent sheisty business partnership, it's all dysfunction. The type of relationship is irrelevant. It's the health of the relationship that matters.

When the relationship becomes irreparably unhealthy you have an #iChoice to make. We'll talk later about how to make intelligent, intentional, inspired, individual choices, or what I've coined #iChoice. How do you know when a relationship is at the irreparably unhealthy stage? You might be the best judge of the health of the relationship, however, many people have been living in dysfunction for so long they have normalized it.

They have *rational lied* their way through it, excusing and overlooking danger signs, red flags and sirens that others on the outside clearly see and hear. The Chinese proverb that says, "A fish can't see the water it is in, unless it jumps out of its fish bowl" is appropriate here. Sometimes we need outside help, like that of a coach, therapist, or mentor to help us see more clearly.

Sometimes we need an #OhSLAP moment—that moment of clarity and keen awareness to realize what is healthy instead of what we've fooled ourselves into believing is OK. One telltale sign of an unhealthy/chronic/degenerative relationship is when your unhappy/bad days far exceed your happy/good days. Whether in a professional or personal relationship, when your positive experience (PosEx) quotient is inverted and your negative experience (NegEx) barometer is increasing and genuine repeated efforts to get back into balance have failed, you just might be in an irreparably unhealthy situation.

By the way, every relationship is a contract with written or unspoken terms and conditions. Relationships are an investment. You give and you get something for what you give. The get has to be equal to or greater than the give for both parties or else someone will eventually feel cheated. The value of what you get is dependent on you and your perspective. In general, for any investment of time, money, resources, if you are not at least breaking even, it is considered a bad investment and you need to cut your loss.

Some ways you know you are in a bad investment (relationship) is when the following occurs.

☆ Your energy level is depleted.

☆ You feel worse about yourself within the relationship than without it.

☆ You go through the motions, not fully engaged, enthusiastic or hopeful.

☆ You hide or avoid interaction.

☆ You skip out on events, call in sick, have more absenteeism.

☆ You spend minimal time on anything involving the relationship.

☆ You stop caring about—all sorts of things—you name it.

☆ You fantasize about your "drop the mic" moment, the day you quit the relationship.

Everyone, everywhere, in all types of relationships implicitly or explicitly apply the "What's in it for me?" test. When there is nothing in the relationship for you other than headache, pain, abuse, insult, irritation, nonsense, lying, discrimination, more work and disrespect, you know this is not a good bargain.

As a fractional part of your relationship, you must always evaluate the value proposition. What value is the other part of the relationship offering to you? Is the value high enough for your time effort and energy? What is the return on investment, effort and energy?

After having evaluated the value proposition of your relationship and doing everything you can to salvage it, you might decide it's time to exit. If that is the choice, you must be prepared. Through lived experiences, I have learned to be prepared before I need to be. You need to always have a plan, a backup plan, and a backup plan to the backup plan.

Here are a few tips, whether you are quitting your job or quitting your family and friends.

☆ Have your own money—always save more than what you think you need.

☆ Have your bag of tricks—know what you can do. What is your talent? Who is in your network? What resources can you access?

☆ Learn to live with essentials—downsize and minimize. What do you really need? You don't need to have a lot of things to live comfortably.

☆ Keep quiet—don't put your business on the street. Not everyone needs to know what you are planning.

☆ Pray for guidance—check your emotions, make sure to practice #iChoice.

☆ Don't be stupid—it's not over 'til it's over—don't count your chickens before they are hatched. In other words, if you are planning to quit your job, make sure you have a legal offer of employment fully executed before you go bragging about it. As a human resources professional, I know that offers of employment can be rescinded.

When I was in a master's degree program in counseling, I learned how to diagnose mental disorders according to the *Diagnostic and Statistical Manual of Mental Disorders.*

Side note: I went to graduate school partly to learn a new profession but mostly because even after being the first person in a family of eight kids to win a full academic scholarship and go to college, I still didn't feel smart enough or adequate enough. Jane was working on my brain, and pursuing a graduate degree was me still trying to prove to Jane that I am smart enough. I would go on to get a second master's degree in international business years later—still trying to prove Jane wrong or gain Jane's approval. I never gained Jane's approval but I finally gained my own. Victory!

During my training I learned that when diagnosing someone with depression, the therapist will assess whether the patient has had a specified number of depressive symptoms for at least two weeks. This diagnostic guide was critical in determining treatment because all of us experience depressive symptoms from time to time. The difference between being clinically depressed and just having depressive moments is the amount of time in either state.

The same goes for unhealthy situations. There might be times when you don't feel as positive about work, life, friends or partners. There might be moments of conflict, disagreement and unhappiness but it doesn't mean the relationship is unhealthy. You need to pay attention and assess whether you are experiencing these situations for a prolonged period of time and determine when to get help and get out.

I've had to make decisions to get out of painful situations a few times. One situation that I vividly recall was a decision to leave a job after uprooting and relocating from my home state hundreds of miles away to take the job. When I arrived to my new environment, I quickly discovered that it was toxic, unwelcoming to me as an outsider and political with a small "p" colloquially known as office politics.

In addition I was faced with a group of "mean girls" who made it their mission to go after a young, smart and attractive outsider. One would think this behavior would end after high school. My enthusiasm for the job, the new adventure and environment was literally met with disdain. Miserable people don't like happy, positive, optimistic people and will work hard to "put you in your place."

The situation became worse each year. No joke, I was either in tears or in a depressed state every day. I cried many nights too. I remember calling my sister frequently, crying and complaining about the situation. She would tell me to just quit and come back home. Not wanting to feel like a failure, I didn't quit.

On Friday nights when most people were happy the work week was over and the weekend finally arrived, I was sad because I knew Monday was coming and I'd have to go back into the lion's den. My stomach hurt. I couldn't enjoy the weekend. I couldn't eat or sleep. I wasn't able to rebound or escape from the malaise. I knew I had to get out. My PosEx was nil; my NegEx was off the charts.

Looking back, I can honestly say that the experience was one of the worst work experiences I've had. Believe it or not, the experience was worse than losing all of my worldly possessions in a wildfire. The wildfire, although tragic, was nature. The job situation with the mean girls was cultivated, deliberate and targeted. It's easy to understand when a tree branch falls and damages your car. It's another thing when someone takes a tree branch and starts to beat your car. You get me?

Despite this horrible experience, I can also say that it was one of the best experiences I've had. Perspective is key to happiness. Although I was in tears most days, I was able to walk away, still standing, still succeeding and achieving. I wasn't broken. I walked away whole. I walked away stronger, wiser and better. I walked away upright, not limping or injured. One of my colleagues gave me a pin-on button as a farewell gift that said, "If you can survive this, you can survive anything." She was correct.

Someone once told me that until the pain of staying the same becomes greater than that of change, you will stay the same. Think about that. You have to decide what your pain threshold is. Have you become comfortable in your discomfort, pain and agony? If you have a high tolerance for pain you might want to modify your threshold.

Just because you can take a blow to the head doesn't mean you should or that it is healthy—especially over the long run—unless of course you're like my shero, Rose Gertrude Namajunas (also known as Thug Rose), an American mixed martial artist. She can take a blow and give a blow . . . but it's her profession, y'all.

When you tolerate pain or stay in a state of agony, physical, mental and spiritual damage is being done whether you can see it or not. Just like shade from a tree won't protect you from sun damage, your ability to withstand greater levels of pain than others won't protect you from emotional damage. There is no badge of honor for repeatedly getting beat down (figuratively or literally).

There is a lot of honor in making the courageous and brave #iChoice to put an end to the beatdowns. Standing up for yourself, against the monster, the giant, the bully and Jane the coward, is honorable. Setting boundaries, establishing standards of treatment and not wavering from them is honorable. It's OK to live by your standards. The people who don't like it are themselves suffering. No healthy person wants you to be unhealthy.

Don't fall into the goody two-shoes trap. Many people tolerate their Jane and stay too long in relationships because they've been taught relationships are hard work. They've been told to stick with it, work it out. Fights and rough patches are normal. Although this is true, they sometimes take these lessons to the extreme.

Dr. Lillian Glass, a California-based communication and psychology expert, is credited for coining the term "toxic people," which is "any relationship [between people who] don't support each other, where there's conflict and one seeks to undermine the other, where there's competition, where there's disrespect and a lack of cohesiveness."

Let's break this down. There are some powerful words and powerful meanings here.

CONFLICT = serious protracted disagreement, a clash
Are you in a long-term clash with anyone?

UNDERMINE = erode, lessen you, bring down
Who is trying to set you up to fail, embarrass you or prove you wrong?

COMPETITION = going up against, a fight
Who is trying to one up or beat you?

DISRESPECT = insult, discredit, disregard
Who is devaluing your voice, dismissing or ignoring you?

LACK OF COHESIVENESS = no unity, peace, connection
Who is creating relational stress, tension, clutter and excess noise?

What relationship in your life right now could be considered toxic? Who is it that you dread to see, work with or be around? Call a thing a thing. You must name it before you can claim your victory. Take a moment to identify your toxic relationships here.

_____

_____

_____

I once received some feedback from a boss who shared that some person who didn't even know me, didn't work for the company I worked at and never had a conversation with me said that I don't care about employees. Because I've been a human resources professional my entire career and have a proven track record of promoting, sponsoring and advocating for opportunities and programs for employees, this was an absurd and out-of-the-blue comment.

I was told that this non-employee person takes every opportunity to make negative comments about me to my boss. Curiously, this person has never made one comment to me. Why is that? What is this person's motivation in bad-mouthing me behind my back? What was their end game? I can think of a lot reasons but for me it boils down to one word—small.

You see, when you are small and want to be big, you tear others down, falsely believing that if you flatten and deflate people with your words you will magically be elevated, pumped up, BIG. Small people are obvious and unoriginal. Small people mind small things.

Confident and courageous people continually mind their mission, mind their business and walk in their greatness. My first thought when I got the news was to say, "Say it to my face, punk." My second and more professional, empathic thought was to say, "Aah, that poor little soul" or as the ole Southern folk say, "Chile, bless his poor soul or heart."

I think it's important to understand why I invoke the soul and heart. The soul is the seat of personality; your will, intellect and emotion all lie in the soul. The word soul means "life." I read once that a healthy mind keeps you focused and engaged. A healthy soul keeps you fulfilled and content.

The heart is the central or innermost part of something.

So when the old folks say, "Bless their soul/heart," they are acknowledging that the offender, the person attempting to discredit and undermine you, is utterly and completely unfulfilled, discontent, empty at their core. It can be an insult or a prayer for their healing because hurt people hurt people. Happy people do not hurt people.

It is human nature to want to react, toss trash back at the person talking trash about you—trying to hurt you. You can make a healthier more empathic #iChoice when you realize they are only trying to hurt you because they see your greatness. They want what you have. Soooo, in a backhanded way they are actually giving you a compliment. Just say thank you and keep doing what you're doing!

When I get feedback like this, I remember what my mother, in her wisdom, told me. She said to first ask myself, "Is any part of what is being said about me true?" If there is *any* truth to what is being said, then by all means decide if you want to make a change. This is called self-reflection and empowerment. It always starts with you.

Most people are so driven by their ego and operate in self-protection mode that they don't even pause to do the reflection. They prefer to deflect instead of reflect. To blame instead of change. To attack and complain instead of face the truth about themselves.

If what is being said about you is untrue (Jane at work again), then my mom said to just smile, correct the record if possible, say thank you and silently or out loud say, "Bless their soul" and keep moving forward.

This advice is golden and applicable in every situation in which Jane tries to provoke you. Continue to let your light shine. Your character, the facts and your work product will speak for you. Over time, Jane will realize that unfounded lies won't and can't stop you. The trash talker will lose credibility or, better yet, disappear, and you didn't have to do anything but just continue to be amazingly you!

Before you decide to end or get away from a toxic environment or relationship, you probably will experience agony over the decision. You toss and turn, asking yourself, friends and even strangers, "What should I do?" The moment you think you have your answer, you begin to question yourself. Doubt and uncertainty creeps in. You feel more confused than ever. The "shoulds" or the "maybes" consume you.

Maybe I should try to work it out. Maybe I should do more. Maybe I should just hang in there. Maybe I should change. Maybe *they will change*. This is the dumbest one of all—especially when it applies to a proven bully or an entire entity.

I'm always amazed when I hear an employee think that an entire organization will change just to meet their needs. I'm equally disturbed when the recipient of regular abuse thinks that the abusive partner will change just for them. People don't change for others. They change for what they will get for that change. If what they get for the change isn't greater than what they believe they have now, or who they believe themselves to be, they will not change.

Staking your happiness on someone else's willingness to change is Jane's best trick. It reminds me of the story of the scorpion and the frog. The author is unknown but you can find various versions of the story on the internet.

• •

A frog was hopping along the shore of a river looking for a place to cross. He came upon a scorpion sitting on the shore.

"Hello, friend frog," said the scorpion. "It appears you are looking to cross the river. I too want to cross. Would you mind carrying me?"

The frog was taken aback. "Why, if I let you on my back to cross the river, you'd sting me and I would die. I don't think I'll do that."

The scorpion immediately replied, "There is no logic to your concern. If I sting you and you die, I will surely die as well, because I can't swim. I wouldn't need a ride if I could swim."

The frog thought a moment and then said, "Your logic makes sense. Why would you kill me if it would result in your death? Come along and climb on my back and we'll cross this river."

The scorpion climbed on the frog's back and off they went to cross the river.

Halfway across the river, the scorpion raised its tail and stung the frog. The frog was both astounded and disconsolate. "Why did you sting me? Now I will die and you will surely drown and die also."

The scorpion replied, "I can't help it. It's who I am. It's in my nature."

• •

There are so many lessons in this little parable. Decisions based *only* on logic or intelligence, emotion or the heart are likely to be the wrong choice. Expecting others to be something that they are not is an exercise in futility.

Let's pause for a moment to reflect: Are you the scorpion or the frog?

_____

_____

_____

Have you ever been stung or tricked by a scorpion? When and why?

_____

_____

_____

Have you ever made a decision—like the frog—against your own better judgment? When and why?

_____

_____

_____

Jane's second best trick, which is closely related to the first trick, is, "Maybe I should be more accepting." That's my favorite—yeah, right! Maybe I should just be more accepting of being a punching bag?! Nope, I'll pass on that, please and thank you. Make no mistake, we've all had a case of the "shoulds." The case of the "shoulds" is a sign of agony.

Agony is a word we don't use every day because it sounds too dramatic, over the top, hyperbolic. I use it here because it's important to fully and accurately describe what you are experiencing and to avoid diluting or diminishing the impact by mislabeling it.

An alcoholic can't say, "I sometimes drink too much." That description doesn't express the gravity of the disease and hinders recovery and treatment. The approach to address someone who might drink too much, eat too much, smoke too much is different than treating someone who has a disease or serious addiction. Call a thing a thing so you can then deal with that thing. A lion is not a house kitty cat and a scorpion is not a cute harmless ladybug that you hope will bring you good luck.

Agony is anguish or mental suffering. It comes when there is misalignment between your spirit and your ego. Your spirit or intuition is speaking gently and lovingly to you, nudging you toward a healthy direction. Your intuition is wise and knowing, however, we rarely hear or heed its wisdom.

The next time you hear yourself using the words should or maybe, assess whether or not you are in doubt or in conflict with what you know to do. For example, I am an introvert. I like my alone time to think, reflect and recharge. It's not only that I like it but also for my personality type, I *need* the alone time.

As a human resources professional, I have to be engaging and interactive with a lot of people (often angry and disgruntled), so evenings and weekends are my haven. I love not having to talk to anyone. The silence is priceless. When friends invite me to a social event occurring during my silent time, 90 percent of the time I know I'd prefer to just stay home. However, I find myself saying, "Maybe I should go," or asking, "Should I go?" I doubt what I know to do, which is to stay at home and recharge.

No one ever has to talk themselves into doing something they want to do. We only try to talk ourselves into doing something we don't want to do but think others think we should do. Whoa! Why is life so complicated? It doesn't have to be once you master #iChoice.

When we are breaking up or ending a situation or deciding to change in some way, we ask these questions, hoping for an easier way out because breaking up, endings and change are hard. Unlike the small quiet voice (spirit), your ego is loud, obnoxious and self-righteous and tells you that you can't quit, you can't leave, you have to stay and make it better, to leave is a sign of weakness, you can't let them win.

Your ego is blind to reality and is unwise. Your ego when unchecked hurts you. Your ego is full of pride and you've heard the saying, "Pride comes before a fall." It has biblical origins from the book of Proverbs but is used today in biblical and secular terms.

I'm not a country singer but I live by Kenny Rogers's advice in "The Gambler."

> You've got to know when to hold 'em
> Know when to fold 'em
> Know when to walk away
> And know when to run

Some relationships you need to go straight to run.

• •

Once there was a beautiful antelope that lived in a forest. He was very proud of his antlers and knew that it helped him look majestic. The antelope would feel very proud whenever other animals stopped by to have a look at him. He always thought that he was a special creation and all the other creatures were no match for him in looks.

But he was always discontented about his legs. He thought his legs were too thin and wished he had better-looking legs. His attitude was so haughty that the other animals did not befriend him at all. No one really liked or respected him although they did agree that he was a very good-looking antelope.

One day as he was quenching his thirst in a lake the antelope suddenly heard the sound of hunters nearby. He had been too busy admiring his reflection in the water that he had not heard the sound of the hunters earlier. Fear gripped him and he ran as fast as he could. The hunters were closing in on him but his legs were so powerful that he was much faster than them.

As he ran through the trees his antlers got caught in the branches of a tree and the antelope could not run further. He struggled to free his antlers and could hear the hunters getting closer. It was then that he realized that what he had all along thought of being his best feature was actually getting him into trouble. Whereas his legs, which he had always looked down on, were actually saving his life.

Luckily with a little struggle the antelope was able to free its antlers from the branches and run to safety. The antelope realized at that moment that its pride had almost cost its life. All along, it had been very proud of its antlers and was blind to the dangers that it might bring about. Now it realized the value of being humble and was happy to be alive. Thereafter the antelope always thought very high of its legs.

• •

The moral of the story? You decide.

Journal Entry

Where is pride/ego interfering with your life?

_____

_____

_____

Self-Assessment

Do you have persistent feelings of unhappiness?
Yes/No

Do you find yourself feeling sad, angry, afraid, anxious, nervous or depressed most of the time?
Yes/No

Do you feel hopeless or like giving in, resigned that this is the way things are?
Yes/No

Are you unable to express joy for others who are happy?
Yes/No

If you answered yes to these questions, you are not alone. I encourage you to seek professional help with a coach or counselor. If you or someone you know is struggling or in crisis, help is available.

24/7 National Crisis Hotline

988 Suicide and Crisis Lifeline

Call, text or chat with trained professionals.

988lifeline.org

If you are ready to release and regroup, the following steps will help you detoxify.

Nine Steps to End Toxic Situations

Step 1—Recognize It Is Toxic

First things first, you have to stop making excuses for other people's actions. Excuses are useless. Stop rational-ly-ing about why you should stay in the relationship or why you aren't leaving (work, relatives/family, partner, etc.).

Excuse
"I can't quit my job even though I'm miserable and things are never going to change because how will I pay my bills?"

Replacement
"I am talented and competent. I know I can find another job where I am valued and appreciated. I will make more than enough to pay my bills and take vacation too! I put my peace of mind first."

Excuse
"Family is family no matter what and although they hurt me, I should never turn my back on them."

Replacement

"I will always love my relatives/family but I will make sure that I do not put myself in harm's way even if that means loving my family from a distance. I put my peace of mind first."

Excuse

"I've known Kathy since we were kids. I know she lies and cheats and is a selfish attention seeker but I can't just dump her, she's my best friend and we have too much history."

Replacement

"Kathy is a dear friend who I will always love. I also love myself and will ensure that I spend time with people who can also love and appreciate me and not always try to compete against me. I put my peace of mind first."

Excuse

"My spouse/partner had a rough life and sometimes they take things out on me. They don't mean to hit or yell at me and I shouldn't take it personally. Love endures all, right?"

Replacement

"Everyone has challenges in life. That doesn't mean they can take it out on me. My spouse/partner will have to decide to get help but I can no longer be the literal or figurative punching bag. I choose self-love and self-care. I put my peace of mind first."

Step 2—
Embrace Total Personal Responsibility

You are the only person who can change you. Start by making #iChoice (intelligent, intentional inspired, individual choices).

Intelligent Choice: You exercise an intelligent choice when you assess and apply all available knowledge and experience and then test that knowledge with the spirit (gut/intuition) before making a decision. You don't let ego, emotions or fear rule the day. You understand, seek and appreciate the wisdom of the inner spirit, and you are not bullied by the obnoxious ego mind.

Intentional Choice: Intentional choice is deliberate, purposeful and made by design. People exercising intentional choice are confident and determined, seeking a specific outcome, while recognizing that the choice they made has a price associated with it. They focus on the reward despite the risk, and they make the choice that is right for them.

Inspired Choice: When a choice is inspired, it springs from deep within. It is often unexplainable but full of certainty. It is different from a mind choice or a heart choice. Your mind and your heart play tricks on you because they depend on the ego. An inspired choice taps into the divine spirit.

Individual Choice: This choice is personal, confident, self-led and emotionally mature people use it. People who understand that at some level they are always in control of what they do, think, feel and behave even though they can't control what others do, think, feel or how they behave. Individual choice makers own their choice once it is made.

Determine what you want in life, and how you want to be. If your current choices are not supporting and advancing these goals, make the decision to change today. That might mean looking for another job, moving out or away, blocking calls. Some actions you will be able to do immediately. Some might take time. For example, don't hastily quit your job before taking the time to plan your next move.

You can do whatever you want but that action might exacerbate your current situation. Instead, play it cool, make the decision you are going to leave and then start your planning. Set a target date to proactively start your search and a target date for resignation. Explore other options that might be available to you financially. Money isn't everything but it is wise to have a backup plan.

I have a friend, Karla T., who was about a year from being eligible to retire with full benefits. The work environment became so toxic for her, she decided to retire early, leaving "money on the table." At the time, I encouraged Karla to find a way to stay that extra year so she could get everything she had earned. I didn't want to see her lose out financially. She was clear on her #iChoice and retired early anyway.

Years later, I asked if she had any regrets. Before I could finish my question she said, "No!"—emphatically. She stated that her mental health and happiness were more important and that she would make the same decision again. Karla T. and I are still friends today—many years after she made that decision. She is happy, enjoying her life and has never looked back. Yes, she might have had to cut down on her expenses but from what I can see, I don't think so.

But people adjust and standard of living is relative. It's amazing how little we need to live comfortably. Eliminating the sometimes twice-daily trips to the fancy coffeehouse, the unnecessary purchase of more clothes, shoes, cable channels, cars or takeout can significantly and immediately provide funds that we thought we didn't have. Karla's actions were unheard of at that time. Today, in the era of the COVID-19 pandemic, this action of putting oneself first over job and money is becoming commonplace.

Bonus: If you can't emphatically and immediately say, "Hell, yes" to an idea, an activity, a thing it's an automatic no. Simple but you have to practice because it goes against our nature to not fit in or do what others want us to do.

Step 3—Remember Who You Are

When you are in an identity crisis, you are like a chameleon changing colors to "fit" in. You change your style, your activities, where you go, who you hang out with. One week it's this. Next week it's that. Whenever you have to do something extra to "fit" in, you are like tissue blowing in the wind, getting momentarily stuck on a bench, a tree branch, and the filthy sidewalk. You become tattered and torn, stepped on, and of little use to you or anyone else.

This isn't you. Remember when you had dreams, ambitions, thoughts of how you wanted your life to be, the people you wanted in your life, the work, hobbies, and activities you wanted to do and the places you wanted to travel to?

Pause for a moment and think back to those days when you were authentically you. Not tainted by someone else's expectations; putting your ideas and the essence of you on the back burner. How do you feel? For some of us, our true self is a distant memory and it might take a bit of work to find. You might need professional help, depending on how long and how well you've hidden yourself. Keep working at it.

As you move Jane out, more of you will be revealed. We are all born with specific gifts, talents and dispositions. We are meant to do good, share our brilliance and contribute to society. Although life can throw us off track, we never permanently lose our divine and inspired gifts; they just get misplaced.

Here are some prompts to help you find you.

What are you naturally good at? List as many things as you can think of.

_____

_____

_____

_____

_____

_____

What do you do that other people marvel at or compliment you on? List all that you can recall.

_____

_____

_____

_____

_____

_____

When you daydream about a better life, what does it include? Be specific. (For example, what are you wearing, what are you doing, who is around you, who is with you, how do you feel, what do you smell?) In other words, use all your senses. Remember, your brain can't tell the difference between reality and imagination. You can create your reality through your imagination.

_____

_____

_____

_____

_____

_____

If money was no object, where would you be right now? What would you be doing? List everything you can think of.

_____

_____

_____

_____

_____

_____

_____

When you leave this earth, what do you want to leave behind? What will be your legacy? List everything you can think of.

_____

_____

_____

_____

_____

_____

What do you want to do before you leave the earth? Why? List everything you can think of.

_____

_____

_____

_____

_____

_____

Knowing your why is important because it will serve as your driver, your motivation and your inspiration. Your why is highly personal, comes from within, so really think about it. Sit quietly and ask yourself why you want to do this or that and wait patiently for the answer to come to you. Write down everything that comes to your mind. Don't judge it, just write it down. You might have lots of things that come to your mind. Examine all of them to see if there are any themes or if there is one that resonates with you the most.

Step 4—Self-Affirmation

The best antidote to your Janes (Yes, you can have more than one Jane. We'll talk about the variations of Jane later.) invading your life is to cut off their oxygen. Your low self-esteem and self-doubt gives life to Jane. The more you build up yourself, your esteem and confidence, the more Jane will take a back seat. Like Kryptonite weakens Superman's powers, your high self-esteem weakens Jane. Bye-bye, Jane and good riddance.

Make no mistake, Jane is always lurking, waiting to be revived, to take front and center. That is why it is important to affirm yourself daily. Notice that the focus is on affirming you and not denouncing Jane. What you resist, persists, so going toe to toe with Jane is futile. Jane will automatically disappear when you take your rightful place, front and center of your life.

Your brain can't accept negative. In other words when you say, "I'm not going to let Jane get in my head," the only thing you will think about is not letting Jane in your head, which Jane already is because you can't stop thinking about Jane.

If you have a Jane in your life, you likely spend too much time trying to soothe Jane's feelings, address their fragility, making sure they aren't in emotional pain and distress. Why? Why do we punish ourselves by accepting fault undeservingly? Women are notorious for this. We comfort, calm and coddle others while dying ourselves, slowly but assuredly. "I'm just a loving person, I care, it's in my nature, or I'm stronger than them, I can take it."

Quit trying to be a hero to those who don't see your bravery, courage, and brilliance. Overextending yourself and trying to please others in this way reduces you to zero—devalues your worth and makes you more invisible.

Almost all behavior is driven by our subconscious brain, which runs on faulty beliefs. Our faulty belief system is so powerful, it allows us to irrationally justify, defend, protect, oddly love, and accept misery and discomfort. To build stronger self-esteem, start with positive affirmations.

Complete the sentences on the next page with one positive word or phrase. Don't worry about if you actually believe or feel that way. For example, I can say I am gifted and able to take on any challenge that life brings. I might not feel that way at the moment but it is how I want to feel, what I want to believe and thus I am positively stating it and claiming it as real.

Once you complete the sentences, repeat them every day, multiple times a day with conviction. This is your daily mantra. Say it out loud, say it in your mind and think about it constantly. As you do this, you will notice that your words/positive affirmations will start to align with your beliefs and feelings. You are creating a new, positive and self-affirming future.

I am_____

I am_____

I am_____

I am_____

I am_____

I am_____

I am_____

I am_____

I am_____

I am_____

Step 5—Establish Guardrails

Breaking bad habits and replacing them with healthier habits takes time, consistency and a lifestyle change. Focusing on what you can't do or won't do is an unnecessary test of human will and is a surefire way to find yourself in the same situation or worse than what you tried to escape. This is why diets, New Year's resolutions and promises don't work.

We will be tempted to seek that which we can't have. This is called psychological reactance. When people feel like their freedom and power of choice is limited or restricted by someone or something, behaviorally they seek to regain their freedom of choice. This might be why some substances, such as marijuana and alcohol that used to be illegal, have now become legal in certain parts of the world. Now that people can have it, they are less likely to go underground and break the law to get it.

People simply don't like to be told they can't have or can't do something. Alternatively, actively making lifestyle changes dependent on a mindset shift exponentially increases your chance of success. In other words, the change becomes who you are and you choose to be, not what you can't do.

To avoid psychological reactance, replace your behavioral restrictions with behavior choice statements.

Restriction
"I will not talk to that person."

Replacement
"I am a person who surrounds myself and engages with individuals who support my goals."

Restriction
"I will not eat junk food."

Replacement
"My body is my temple and I treat it with respect, nourishing it daily with things that support my health."

Restriction
"I will not spend money on that dress."

Replacement
"I am a person who uses my money wisely, focusing on building assets versus liabilities. I reward myself for my hard work and for reaching my goals."

Restriction
"I will not be disrespected."

Replacement
"I am a person worthy of respect. I will respect others and model and communicate how I'd like to be treated with others. I will speak up for myself as an act of self-love."

Step 6—Embrace the Stages of Change

People reliably respond to change in the same way. Whether graduating from high school and moving into early adulthood, getting married or divorced, or retiring from a long career, people experience similar emotions. There is always a feeling of loss and expectancy, fear and hope, a bit of sadness and excitement when going through change.

In high school, I remember wanting to hurry up and graduate so I could get on with my life. I was so eager and excited to become a self-sufficient adult, go to college, meet new friends and get a career. I went to summer school just so I could graduate in three years. On graduation day, I remember the pomp and circumstance, people all dressed up, families and friends there to celebrate with me, my classmates hugging one another, saying goodbye and "let's stay in touch" knowing that we might never see one another again.

I recall crying and being sad that this chapter that I worked so hard to reach, that my glorious high school days, was over. Such a paradox! I wanted it to be over, I worked hard at accelerating its end, yet I was terribly reminiscent and longing for what was when that day actually came.

Most people have the same mixture of feelings—sadness, loss, desire to look backward, longing for the "good ole days," or hope and elation for what the future might hold. These responses hold true for kicking Jane to the curb.

There is a certain comfort, albeit unhealthy, in staying in discomfort and dysfunction.

As humans we can adapt to myriad miserable experiences and learn to tolerate them overtime. When faced with giving up our misery, it can yield sadness. You might feel sad for what could have been or what you hoped for. You might feel sad for what you had become and how far you've strayed from your essence. You might feel sad that you wasted so much time not fulfilling your dream.

Sadness or variations of it (depression/anger) are normal and should be expected, welcomed and explored. Sadness will visit you like the irritating relative at Christmastime but, just like your relatives, the emotion will leave eventually. Know that sadness and other emotions are a part of the process toward self-love, courage and self-esteem and it cannot be skipped. Be assured that you will get through it.

Step 7—Increase Your Mental Health Outlet (MHO)

Lisa M. Sanchez, friend, author of *Looking for Love in a Garbage Can: A Journey of Healing—How I Survived an Alcoholic Environment* and my business partner of *The Positive Platform: Lifting and Living with Lisa and Lori*, has taught me the value of MHO. She coined this phrase during the COVID-19 pandemic as a reminder of self-care, self-love and self-healing during unusually stressful and uncertain times.

I love great ideas packaged in memorable ways, so I've adopted MHO into my own practice. Lisa's MHO is taking a walk every day, listening to reggaeton music. This brings her joy and helps her to stay balanced throughout the day.

I have a bucket of MHOs, depending on the situation. I might disconnect completely (turn off electronics and meditate, take a drive blasting my music, hike the mountain or watch a sad/heartwarming movie to elicit tears (crying is a great MHO).

What's your MHO? List as many as you can think of here.

My MHO

_____

_____

_____

_____

_____

_____

_____

Step 8—Keep Looking Forward

When you leave a situation, it is human nature to want to look back. Looking back or going back is a dangerous proposition. *Side note: Taking a step back to regroup is different from going back.* One thing that the world's dumbest criminals have in common is returning to the scene of the crime. OMG!

What about the Bible story of Lot's wife who turned into a pillar of salt after looking back in the midst of fleeing from town? The dumb criminal and Lot's wife's fate were not good. Looking backward leads to destruction. Looking forward leads to gain. There are a few occasions when looking back is beneficial, for example, when you look back to measure your progress or how far you've come. If you look back too soon, you might be tempted to turn around.

I love to hike. It is my happy place. I don't choose the hikes that are the equivalent of a stroll through the park. My kind of hiking is vigorous, challenging and gets the heart rate up within thirty seconds due to the immediate and never-ending incline.

There is one trail in the Santa Monica Mountains in California that I love to hike. As soon as I start the hike, I'm exhausted. After a few bends and turns, I can see far, far ahead to where I will arrive if I stay the course.

The mountain is splattered with neon green, orange, pink and yellow dots bobbing along the trail. I'm envious because these dots are the lucky hikers ahead of me. I am regretful that I didn't start my hike sooner, because it means I would be closer to ending the bodily torture that I'm putting myself through. Nevertheless, I keep a steady and laborious pace forward.

At a certain point during every hike, when I'm not even halfway up but it feels like it, I question, should I just make this a short hike today? I can turn around now and go back. After forcing myself to just keep putting one foot in front of the other, I finally reach the pinnacle.

I look back, appreciative that my perseverance and progress led to the prize. I am always grateful that I didn't listen to Jane telling me, "You don't need to do this today." When I stay the course, I feel great satisfaction. The joy and scenic beauty of nature is always worth the effort.

Step 9—Apply What You've Learned

People say knowledge is power. Wrong. Knowledge without application is futile. Don't mistake activity for action or progress. Activity without intentional focus is regression, not progression. If you are not moving forward, you are by default moving backward. You might think that you are "resting in place" but everyone else around you who is applying their knowledge is moving forward, leaving you farther behind. There is no such thing as "resting in place."

Repeat, repeat, repeat your positive affirmations. Get an accountability partner. Measure your progress against your own best self. Ask yourself, "Am I better today than yesterday? Am I practicing #iChoice? How is my energy and vibe? Am I happier, more at peace, enthusiastic more days than not?" Yes? Good, this is progress. No? Don't fret. Regroup, recalibrate and start from now.

Now means now. Not tomorrow and not five minutes from now. If you are reading this book, please pause from reading and do what you need to do to make a shift now. It can be as simple as reciting your positive self-affirmations. You will have good days and bad. Reexamine your PosEx against your NegEx. Change the balance of the two and change your life.

This chapter was about regrouping (getting yourself together) after the breakup. If you are reading this book and not actually pausing to do the reflective exercises, you are not applying what you are learning. If you break up but choose to keep or hold on to certain aspects of the relationship, you are not applying what you've learned.

Keeping old furniture, gifts, the old circle of friends, the negative messages, and the self-criticism will keep you stuck. Give that jewelry back and buy your own ring. When you break up you might find it best to do as my friend Karla T. did. In essence she said, "You keep your money and toxic environment and I'll take my peace of mind, my joy, my future." Door slammed and locked.

There are multiple new and exciting doors to open. Too many of us don't make the clean break and we leave space to revert back to the old state of being. Not the best move. Click, click, click that door shut.

Chapter 3:

Redirect—
What Do I Do Now?

Redirect/rēdə'rekt

Verb

"Direct (something) to a new or different place or purpose. Change their course or destination."

—*Oxford Languages, Collins English Dictionary*

Redirect

Are you ready for the next chapter in your life? I don't mean writing about it but actually living it. I don't know about you but I want my next chapter to be a page-turner; full of excitement, freedom, friendship and happiness. Like a good book that you can't stop reading, I don't want to stop going forward, living and pursuing the life I want and deserve. It's exciting to be on a path toward something new; going to a different place with a renewed purpose. If you are ready for a change, you have to decide to move on. You have been redirected.

Have you ever had someone throw up all over you? Not literally, that would be utterly disgusting. I mean they vomit misguided anger at you that you knew was less about you than the person's own insecurity, fear and pressure.

In the past I would handle those situations in kind, meeting volatility with volatility. Like Easy-E rapped in his song "It's On"—"If it's on, mother*cker, then it's on." I like the song—the beat mostly. The lyrics and the message not so much. The song is about a beef Eazy-E has with Snoop Dogg and Dr. Dre. The song escalates matters versus resolves them.

However, being honest with you, I sometimes feel the need to code switch—the practice of alternating between two or more languages or varieties of language in a conversation or situation. I feel that sometimes you have to show someone a different side of you to make a point.

I have a bachelor's degree in interpersonal communication. For communication to be effective, you have to know your audience and adjust accordingly. Polite communication doesn't work with everyone. Remember what I said about bullies earlier in this book? Getting rid of Jane might not be as easy as a nice polite letter or conversation. You might have to show Jane that you mean business.

Colorful language helps. Some might call it going gangsta. I've had to "go gangsta" a few times with the Janes in my life, just to make sure they knew I wasn't the one to be messed with. It didn't make me feel good and it isn't the way I want to show up in this life. So I decided to ask, "How's my approach working out?"

It wasn't working. I then tried a different approach. Still feeling like I was on defense—I tried the explanation approach. Eagerly trying to make the angry person understand my point of view. "Please understand me because deep down inside I want you to really like me and I don't want you to be mad at me. I know that I didn't really do anything to warrant the vomit but I'll take it if it means you will still be my friend."

Barf! That didn't work either. It just gave Jane a boost. The more you try to please a Jane, the stronger and more false confidence Jane feels and this strength is reflected in Jane's attacks. Confidence built on someone else's demise is false confidence.

Today my approach is much different. Some would call it hysteria, whispering, "She's gone stone cold mad." I choose to call it crazy confidence. When I get a yell out from anyone—I laugh and laugh and laugh—silently of course. To laugh out loud would be—well—just rude. The bubble above my head reads, "Are you kidding me right now? Are you really trying to dress me down over a trivial issue that won't matter five minutes, five days or five weeks from now?" Then I channel my inner Italian—"Git outta here" followed by the words of female rapper Nicki Minaj, "Yes, I did, yes, I did. Somebody please tell him who the eff I is."

I got a yell out one day from a boss who was not qualified to be in the position but, due to various suspicious organizational incidents, landed in the role. As a fully-grown woman with more years of professional work experience than that person, the behavior caught me off guard at first and I was like *Whaaat*? Is this really happening? I felt like the Baudelaire children in *Lemony Snicket's A Series of Unfortunate Events*.

I had to look around to see if I was being punk'd. Bullies take punk shots, you know. Nope, no hidden cameras, Ashton Kutcher or Chance the Rapper in sight. But my age, coupled with wisdom gained along my journey, allowed me to just listen instead of react. By listening I was able to see the pain, fear and anxiety that they were feeling at the moment. The issue was so stupid and the reaction so over-the-top, I knew it couldn't possibly be about me.

In the past, I would have internalized and attributed this treatment to something I had done but not today. I knew it was about their fear of inadequacy, of being criticized for not being perfect, of being out of control and of people realizing that they are an imposter, posing as someone who could lead. I let the vomit flow, nonplussed, mind you, and said, "OK, let me see what I can do to make the situation better."

In this instance, because it was clear to see the motivation behind the vomit—which was sheer and utter fear—I moved into solutions mode. "Let me help you with *your* problem." I emphasized "your" problem because it was not my problem.

I learned this technique years ago when I was a leadership trainer and did a workshop based on C. W. Metcalf's video series titled *Humor, Risk and Change.* The video reminds the viewer to not take themselves too seriously and to disconnect from the issue so they can focus on the problem and not themselves.

I chose not to take this on, like I would have in the past. I didn't internalize it, question and doubt myself, beat myself up, lament over it for days and engage in negative self-talk, such as "How can I be so stupid?" I didn't feel rejected or dejected. Those days are long gone.

When people try to throw you-know-what at me, I just step to the side and keep moving. I don't step in it or walk around with their stuff on me. In this case, I rejected the rejecter. My rejection of Jane's nonsense was a positive redirection toward increasing my PosEx.

Side note: When people vomit on you **they** *are sick . . . not you.*

I've had many Janes in my life. If you're a nice, kind, loving, professional person like moi, Janes might be hard to spot at first, but rest assured, they will find you. They are a type of bully and bullies are notorious for sniffing out people they perceive as "weak." They find the innocent, people minding their own business.

To bullies, kindness is perceived as license to abuse. They feel so deeply insecure and inadequate and the temporary antidote is to target someone else perceived as smaller so they can feel bigger. You might find yourself catering to the bully by asking, "Can I take your load of crap off of you? Can I ease your discomfort? No, no, don't worry about me. Yes, I'm uncomfortable too but that's OK, I can take it."

You might find that Janes are readily found in the workplace. Someone is always trying to point fingers, find a scapegoat, and keep their hands clean, cover their arse. Jane is like a pimp taking advantage of, exploiting or using people for their own benefit. Jane is always seeking someone to pimp out. You don't want to be Jane's lapdog, to put it kindly.

Call me crazy, but I have learned to love rejection. Don't get me wrong. No one understandably wants to feel rejected all the time, but I've learned that rejection is not a commentary of my worth yet it is a strong signal that I am worth more and better.

We often think too small. We pursue a job, a relationship and an opportunity that we think is in our league instead of at the level we really deserve. Our subconscious belief system drives our behavior so if we subconsciously believe that we are only worth X, we seek X. However, the universe (if you are open to it) is on your side, conspiring to bring goodness to you. And although you seek X, X rejects you. Thank goodness, because X++ is waiting for you right around the corner.

This has happened to me more times than I can count. I apply for a job I really want. I make it far into the process and when it's down to me or the other person, the organization chooses the other person. I fall in love with an apartment or home I want to purchase. I put a bid on the property but the owner selects someone else. Sad, dejected, hurt and disappointed are natural reactions.

Feeling sorry for myself and full of self-doubt, I ruminate on all sorts of low base thoughts, such as maybe I'm not what they were looking for. I'm not as good as I think I am. What's wrong with me? What am I doing wrong? Am I being discriminated against?

These feelings and thoughts can be consuming when you don't understand that rejection is simply divine redirection. Undoubtedly, every time without fail when X rejected me, I obtained a bigger, better prize. I've learned to embrace and leverage everything. Setbacks are a great setup for huge comebacks. Think about it. When you need to leap over a tall building, you have to take several steps back to get up and over.

The flip side of the equation is when your ego gets in the way and you refuse to accept the lifeline offered to you. You are hell-bent on getting X and you pursue, fight and scratch until you get it. Then you find out that the sack of gold you thought you were fighting for was only a sack of coal. Oops. You are miserable and don't want to keep your catch. Like a person who is fishing, you want to throw the boot (or partner, job, car, opportunity) back into the sea.

Can you relate? Ever fought for and caught something and quickly realized you didn't want it? You got caught up in the chase. Your pride wouldn't let you lose but you lost anyway. We've all wished that the thing we thought we wanted and eventually obtained got away instead.

This must be what is meant in the lyrics "The One That Got Away" sung by The Civil Wars.

> I got caught up by the chase
> And you got high on every little bit
> I wish you were the one
> Wish you were the one that got away
>
> Oh, if I could go back in time
> When you only held me in my mind
> Just a longing, gone without a trace
> Oh, I wish I never ever seen your face
> I wish you were the one
> Wish you were the one that got away

Sadly, people in this conundrum stay in the situation because they feel stuck or too embarrassed to admit they made a mistake. They fail to realize that there is always a way of escape. You are never truly stuck. Sure, you might have to start over, eat humble pie or take a series of small steps and maneuvers to break free. The wise know that small steps will eventually get you there. Where? Wherever you want to go!

Whenever I feel stuck, I follow these three steps.

Step 1: Believe that you are not stuck.

Change starts in the mind and manifests in your actions. You might feel stuck but you have to tell yourself that you are not. Call on the universe, your divine intelligence, to bring you the answer for your first move. Your first move might be so small it is imperceptible to anyone. I call them microscopic moves. However, you know that you've made a shift that will create more shifts until you are free.

Your beliefs are largely driven by your subconscious mind and they drive behavior, attitude and outcomes. If you find yourself repeating the same old habits, falling prey to the same traps, accepting the same poor treatment at work, with friends, family or strangers, you are largely the cause of these experiences. The common denominator is you.

Think about it. Can everyone in the world who you encounter really be against you? Unlikely. So the question you must ask yourself is, "What am I doing to manifest my undesirable reality?" There is freedom simply in taking control of you—which is the only thing you have control over. To get untangled faster, first start with you. If you are expecting others to change to meet your needs, buckle in and start counting the years of continued unhappiness.

Step 2: Get up and make a move.

The direction you move is irrelevant as long as it is not backward. Remember what I said earlier. A step back is not the same as going back. When you are driving to a location and you accidently pass your turn by a bit, you back up just a little so you can make the turn. It's a small adjustment. You don't make a U-turn and go back home.

The key is to just move from the spot you're in. It can be up, down, left or right. Don't worry about what comes after the first move. You don't need to have all the answers upfront. The next step will be revealed to you. Trust in the process.

To make the first move simply ask yourself, "What is the one action that I can take today to change my circumstance?" It could be as simple as getting out of bed, making a phone call, researching an item, establishing a budget, taking a self-assessment, taking a class, writing down a vision of what you want, reading a book, getting a coach, meditating, praying, seeing a therapist, exercising. The list can go on forever.

You must ask the question first and then listen for the

answer. It will come. Ask the critical question in the form of "What can I . . . or how can I . . . ?" Your brain is a creative problem solver. When you ask a question, its job is to go to work, scouring for a solution. Neuroscientists—people who study the brain and how it impacts behavior—say that questions act as a catalyst for our brains.

When you ask a question, the brain activates and releases serotonin, a chemical that carries messages between nerve cells in the brain and throughout your body. It allows you to relax and the relaxation encourages intelligence gathering from all areas of the brain, giving you insight and solutions.

I was inspired by Robert Kiyosaki's message in his book, *Rich Dad Poor Dad*, to pursue passive income through real estate. I remember reading his book years ago lying by the pool at a hotel in Singapore of all places. I had some free time because I was actually there for a leadership conference that got canceled after my arrival. I was already there and the event was paid for so I stayed and enjoyed exploring the country (I was redirected).

The Oh SLAP moment—the sobering moment of clarity as defined in my book *Oh SLAP! My Choices Determine My Destiny!*—was when I realized that the way to find solutions to problems is in the way you pose the problem statement. Robert Kiyosaki's advice was instead of saying, "I can't afford it," you should ask, "How can I afford it?"

This line of questioning is like magic. Asking that open-ended question activated my brain to go and find the answer.

The first statement, "I can't afford it," automatically shuts the brain off, deactivates it. I can't, therefore I won't. This leaves you in status quo.

Think of your brain as a laptop computer. When you hit the start button, it lights up, scans the system for viruses, pops up various apps and suggested products you might need. It is ready to work for you. Your brain is ready to work for you but you need to push the on button.

Step 3: Keep moving, and don't look back.

Clarity comes as you move forward. It might seem scary at first but you must trust the process. Think of a huge stairwell that is dimly lit. All you see at ground zero is the first step of the stairwell. Steps two through a thousand are hidden, dark and spooky. You can't see the end of the stairwell and you don't know if it bends and curves left or right. You don't know how long it will take you to arrive at the top of the stairwell or if you ever will arrive (life is a journey not a destination after all).

Imagine yourself taking the first step that you can barely see. You steady yourself on that one step, checking to make sure you are OK and safe and you realize, "Hmm, I'm actually OK. Let me try taking the next step." Each step you take sheds a bit more light on the next step. It might be a slow and laborious process and you wish you could just flip the switch and see every step all at once.

But aah, life is a mystery and this step-by-step process is

necessary for you to establish greater levels of faith, confidence, security, hope and power. You will start to say, "I'm not sure where I'm going but I know I'm going up."

What is the first step you see on your staircase? Write it down below. As you take that first step, more clarity is achieved, and you keep moving up the staircase.

This is my step one on the staircase.

_____

_____

I will take this first step on _____

Side note: *Now is best.*

Chapter 4:

Recover—
It's OK, I've Got This

Recover/rɪˈkʌvər/
Noun

"Return to a normal state of health, mind, or strength. Find or regain possession of (something stolen or lost)."
—*Encyclopedia.com*

Recover

Yesterday I woke up confused. At the thought of you I felt anger, anxiety and frustration. I was in tears. Your horribleness consumed me. I couldn't shake it. I couldn't sleep, work or concentrate. I'm sure you had no idea or concern because as a Jane you are incapable of recognizing the carnage you leave behind.

I was emotionally unhealthy, out of control yet still trying to please you. I realized that I unwittingly allowed you to take from me what was rightfully mine—my joy, peace and happiness.

I listened to the lyrics to "Recovery" sung by James Arthur and it moved me to tears. I could only think about what the songwriter was going through when this song was written. Undoubtedly, there was a Jane lurking in the mind of the songwriter.

I realized that to recover, I could no longer blame you. I have seized back what was taken. I am protective of what I own. Don't even think about playing this game with me again. I am stronger now. I am more resolved and determined. Game over.

As James Arthur sings, "I don't wanna play this game no more." The lyrics to his song are so powerful; I'm sharing a portion here with the hope that it will resonate in your soul as it did me.

I don't wanna play this game no more
I don't wanna play it
I don't wanna stay 'round here no more
I don't wanna stay here
Like rain on a Monday morning
Like pain that just keeps on going on

Look at all the hate they keep on showing
I don't wanna see that
Look at all the stones they keep on throwing
I don't wanna feel that
Like sun that will keep on burning
I used to be so discerning, oh

In my recovery
I'm a soldier at war
I have broken down walls
I defined, I designed
My recovery
In the sound of the sea
In the oceans of me
I defined, I designed
My recovery

Today I woke up happy. I saw you in a room the other day.
I didn't tremble. My emotions didn't go wild with anxiety,

frustration or anger. I looked at you and felt nothing. You no longer have power over me. I continued to smile and laugh at the beauty around me. My inner joy consumed me. You are not part of my joy. You are not part of my misery.

I exist as a complete, whole, healthy person. I choose selectively who enters my orbit. You had the chance; you could have shared space with me. You blew it, Jane. The situation today is just perfect without you. Without you, I've made room for other more worthy beings.

One day you too will wake up feeling free—if you do the work. One day you will stop letting Jane occupy your brain. You will not let insane Jane stay in your brain all night, dwelling on what they did or did not do, what they said or did not say. You will step back and examine why you were presented with the gift of Jane.

Perspective is a choice and positive perspective is a gift. It plays a crucial role in recovery. As awful as Jane is, Jane turned out to be a gift just wrapped in ugly paper. Jane made it necessary for you to seize back your power. Understanding that things aren't happening *to* you but happening *for* you is mind-blowing and life-changing.

If you believe things are happening to you, then you become a victim, subject to Jane's abuse. If you believe that things happen for you, you can embrace your experiences with confidence knowing that in the end you win. I love the beginning of DJ Khaled's song "All I Do Is Win." "All I do is win, win, win, no matter what." Now that's what I call positive perspective.

You don't have time to waste; you don't have space to give to unproductive people and thoughts. If the situation won't matter five minutes, five days or five months from now, let it go. It's 5:15 (five times three) somewhere. That's happy hour to me. Positive perspective.

There is a freedom that comes with age, although I'm not "old" by economist's standards that claim people will live to more than 110 years old. The point is that the older you get, the less you care about how you appear to others. No more pretense, no more façades. Cracks, flaws, quirks are trumpeted proudly and confidently. You've earned it. Someone doesn't like it? Oh, well—too bad for them. I woke up happy today!

There's a quote floating around on social media that says, "When you're twenty, you care what everyone thinks; when you're forty, you stop caring what everyone thinks; when you're sixty, you realize no one was ever thinking about you in the first place." Regardless of who said this, there is merit it to it. You don't have to wait to hit these age milestones.

You can decide right now to stop thinking about others and become unapologetically self-centered. Self-centeredness is not to be confused with selfishness. To be self-centered means to be grounded, sure of self, confident, focused and at peace. You don't let Jane distract you. You don't let Jane take your power away.

You recognize that if Jane lashes out, criticizes or points the finger at you, it is more about Jane and Jane's pain than about you. Perhaps it is Jane's jealousy and envy. These two emotions are similar but different and invade every relationship you will ever be in.

Jealousy is a feeling of resentment, bitterness or hostility toward someone who has something that you don't have. This could be general success, an achievement, a trait, a social advantage, a material possession or a relationship, among other things. What matters is that the other person has the thing, you want it, and this makes you resentful of them.

Envy is a negative feeling of desire centered on someone who has something that you do not. *Envy* implies that you want to be in the other person's position—to have what they have. *Envy* can be described as a mix of admiration and discontent.

I contend that a person's jealousy or envy is based on their fear and insecurities derived from their faulty belief system. Deep down they believe they are lacking. If you are doing well in an area or have something that Jane wants but doesn't have, Jane interprets this as failure.

Jane believes they are not doing well in comparison to you. They believe they are falling short—but that's because they are using the wrong measuring stick. More important, they feel that their disposition is a fait accompli, that it cannot change. This makes them resentful.

Although people are jealous and envious over tangible and intangible things, I've noticed that the deepest resentment is based on intangible things, not possessions. For example, if you have a positive outlook on life, are in a good mood all the time, have a nice smile, if people want to be around you or you have natural internal and external beauty, Jane really hates you. Why?

The intangible things are a reflection of your essence and inner being. They cannot be purchased. They cannot be replicated or duplicated. They can't even be imitated. Tangible material things are less threatening to people because they can easily compete with you on those things (clothes, houses, cars)—even if it means going into debt to get it.

It's hard to compete with someone's essence. But why is Jane competing with you in the first place? That is the problem. Jane, focus on you and stop focusing on me, please.

Jealousy is poisonous and destructive. It is indicative of a poverty mindset. It's a belief and attitude that you will never have or be enough. You focus more on what others have that you don't instead of being grateful for what you have. You can shift from a poverty mindset to a prosperity mindset if you choose to.

Sarah Prout—bestselling author, podcaster, manifestation expert and cofounder of *Dear Universe*—identified ten ways that prosperity mindsets think differently and how you can start adopting these traits to change your destiny.

These two are my favorites.

★

Prosperity Mindsets are conscious and mindful.

★

"People with prosperity mindsets are consciously aware of their actions and the impact they will have. If something could harm themselves or others, they steer clear of going in that direction."

★

Prosperity Mindsets let go of limiting beliefs.

★

"A prosperity mindset will open their heart and examine the beliefs that are holding them back. The purest form of this mindset is dedicated to consistent personal development and growth."

As you kick your Jane to the curb in your recovery, my only hope for all Janes is that they too find their own recovery.

Chapter 5:

Rebuild—Hello John

Rebuild/rē'bild/
Verb

"To build (something) again after it has been damaged or destroyed."
—*The Britannica Dictionary*

Hello John Letter

A letter written to start a new, fresh, positive relationship or opportunity. John can be a gender-neutral person, place or thing but in my case it is my husband to be. John represents Joy, Opportunity, Happening, Now!

Rebuild

If breaking up is hard, rebuilding can be even harder. It can be arduous, laborious, frustrating and exhausting. No one really thrives on rebuilding except for kids. Remember when you were a kid and you didn't do so well in a game? You lost the game and the first thing you wanted was a do-over. You failed a test and you begged the teacher for a do-over. Your Easy-Bake Oven cake didn't bake and you just made another one. You wrecked your science fair project or your homemade go-kart or your bike and you just scrounged around for the material to rebuild it.

Rebuilding simply isn't a big deal when you are ten years old. It's a different ordeal when you are over forty. At ten, do-overs gave you hope for a better outcome. It was a challenge and exciting as you competed against other kids and your previous performance to win. Additionally, you had your parents pushing you to try again.

As good parents, that's what they are supposed to tell you. They don't want their kid to become a quitter; giving up forever after one disappointment, loss or failure. It's strange how as years pass, the enthusiasm for do-overs is replaced with "No, thank you" and "I don't, I can't, I won't do that again." It's strange how the good advice adults give to kids is advice they no longer follow themselves.

Have you ever been fired from a job after spending many years working for the company? The first thing you think of is what you are going to do, because you don't want to start over.

According to divorce attorneys and researchers, almost 50 percent of all marriages in the United States will end in divorce or separation. And 41 percent of all first marriages end in divorce. After the investment of building a life with someone, acquiring assets, having children, sharing hopes and dreams all to be dashed with a declaration by one or both parties of irreconcilable differences, few people rush for a do-over.

Maybe you've lost your home and everything in it, like I did a few years back in a California wildfire. Maybe you've lost a personal or professional connection for whatever reason—death, divorce, disagreement. You have choices. Darren Hardy, author and self-improvement mentor, says that what you did, what you didn't do but know that you should have done and how you responded to what happened have created every outcome in your life.

Regardless of whether you accept this fully or not, you have choices. You can wallow in victimhood. Throw in the towel. Give up, give in and lose. Or you can get up, change course.

Choice 1

This is the easy choice. It's easy to wallow in self-pity. Our society seems prone to entitlement and to blaming others when something undesirable happens or people don't get what they feel entitled to. People in this mode never seem to look inward to find strength from within. They don't embrace their inner greatness and power. They never seem to look up to find hope from above, to tap into a power greater than themselves. They seem to find likeminded people who will validate their faulty belief system that they are nothing more than chickens pecking at seeds and crumbs on the ground versus soaring like the great and mighty eagles that there are.

The fable of the eagle and the chicken says it best.

• •

A fable is told about an eagle that thought he was a chicken. When the eagle was very small, he fell from the safety of his nest. A chicken farmer found the eagle, brought him to the farm, and raised him in a chicken coop among his many chickens. The eagle grew up doing what chickens do, living like a chicken, and believing he was a chicken.

A naturalist came to the chicken farm to see if what he had heard about an eagle acting like a chicken was really true. He knew that an eagle is king of the sky. He was surprised to see the eagle strutting around the chicken coop, pecking at the ground, and acting very much like a chicken. The farmer explained to the naturalist that this bird was no longer an eagle. He was now a chicken because he had been trained to be a chicken and he believed that he was a chicken.

The naturalist knew there was more to this great bird than his actions showed as he "pretended" to be a chicken. He was born an eagle and had the heart of an eagle, and nothing could change that. The man lifted the eagle onto the fence surrounding the chicken coop and said, "Eagle, thou art an eagle. Stretch forth thy wings and fly." The eagle moved slightly, only to look at the man; then he glanced down at his home among the chickens in the chicken coop where he was comfortable. He jumped off the fence and continued doing what chickens do. The farmer was satisfied. "I told you it was a chicken," he said.

The naturalist returned the next day and tried again to convince the farmer and the eagle that the eagle was born for something greater. He took the eagle to the top of the farmhouse and spoke to him: "Eagle, thou art an eagle. Thou dost belong to the sky and not to the earth. Stretch forth thy wings and fly." The large bird looked at the man, then again down into the chicken coop. He jumped from the man's arm onto the roof of the farmhouse.

Knowing what eagles are really about, the naturalist asked the farmer to let him try one more time. He would return the next day and prove that this bird was an eagle. The farmer, convinced otherwise, said, "It is a chicken."

The naturalist returned the next morning to the chicken farm and took the eagle and the farmer some distance away to the foot of a high mountain. They could not see the farm or the chicken coop from this new setting. The man held the eagle on his arm and pointed high into the sky where the bright sun was beckoning above. He spoke: "Eagle, thou art an eagle! Thou dost belong to the sky and not to the earth. Stretch forth thy wings and fly." This time the eagle stared skyward into the bright sun, straightened his large body, and stretched his massive wings. His wings moved, slowly at first, then surely and powerfully. With the mighty screech of an eagle, he flew.

• •

Moral of the Story

- -

☆ Know who you are.

☆ Don't let anyone treat you like something you are not.

☆ Don't do what the crowd does.

☆ Heed the call to do and be better.

☆ Don't look back, don't go back.

☆ Sometimes you have to change your surroundings and go far away to find your true self.

What others lessons did you learn from this fable?

_____

_____

_____

_____

_____

_____

_____

_____

_____

Choice 2

This takes a bit more effort. You can choose to get up, get moving and rebuild bigger and better.

This is sometimes easier said than done. It takes effort, it takes commitment and it takes an inner belief system that things can change for the better.

We can learn a lesson from Uma Thurman's character, whose codename is Black Mamba in *Kill Bill: Volume* 1. There is a scene where Black Mamba wills herself to wiggle her toes so that she can drive away in a stolen car after awaking from a coma and escaping from a hospital. Her atrophied legs were not working but she focused on her vision (to gain access to her mobility) and repeatedly commanded her feet to move.

It's a powerful scene to watch her in a powerless state to command power. You and I have that same ability. There have been many dark days when I was not immobilized physically but imprisoned mentally and emotionally. I had to repeatedly command myself to get up and walk out of the prison of my own mind. Just as Black Mamba said, "Wiggle your big toe. Wiggle your big toe. Wiggle your big toe." I had to repeat a command to myself.

Self-Reflection
Journal Entry

In order for you to rebuild, what commands do you have to repeat?

_____

_____

_____

_____

_____

_____

_____

_____

Your repeated power command will yield great results taking you from point A to point B. It will position you to finally say goodbye to Jane and the low self-esteem inducing messages and say Hello John—Joy, Opportunity, Happening, Now.

Chapter 6:

Remember—
Don't Repeat

Remember/rImEmbUH/
Verb

"Be able to bring to one's mind an awareness of (someone or something that one has seen, known, or experienced in the past)."
—*Oxford Languages*

Remember

Forgiveness of yourself and others is necessary for a productive, prosperous life. Never forgetting where you've been and how far you've come is essential to continued success, courage and confidence. Once you know what and how to do better and don't do it, you have chosen to stay connected to Jane.

An action done once or twice could be considered to be a mistake. The same action done three or more times is a choice. Doing the same thing over and over again and expecting different results is insanity.

We all have the right to live our lives how we please. My goal in writing the series of self-leadership and self-empowerment books is to help those who want to be helped choose differently, make #iChoices and change the course of their lives.

Writing a Dear Jane letter just might be one of the most difficult things you need to do. There are many types of Janes so you will need to decide where to start first.

Jane Type 1—That Job

Coworkers, peers, employees, supervisors are overly critical. You receive targeted scrutiny. People jump at the first opportunity to discredit and undermine you. The people and organizational culture is toxic, passive-aggressive, cutthroat. You are working hard but feel you are in a state of churn, not achieving or moving forward. It's chaotic and exhausting.

What can you do to break up with Jane Type 1?

Dear Jane

_____

_____

_____

_____

_____

_____

_____

_____

_____

Jane Type 2—Those Relatives

You've got some Janes in your family. Who is it? Is it your parents, siblings, cousins who always have something negative to say about you or others? They are gossipy, spreading information that tears down instead of lifts up. Do they ridicule you, try to make you feel ashamed for your success? Are they unaccepting of your lifestyle and choices?

I separated from certain members of my family for twenty years. It was necessary for my healing and mental strength. Two decades sound over the top but it was the only way I could forgive and then reconcile and reconnect with my family as a more confident, happy person with clear boundaries.

What can you do to break up with Jane Type 2?

Dear Jane

_____

_____

_____

_____

_____

_____

Jane Type 3—
Not So Friendly Friends

Does it seem that you are the one giving to your friends? Do you initiate compliments and never or rarely have it reciprocated? Do you find yourself bending to meet your friends' constant need for attention, approval and praise while never getting the same back? This is depleting and unbalanced. Any close connection, friend or family who doesn't offer basic well wishes but expects it from you or can't genuinely celebrate every celebratory moment in your life is a Jane.

Be aware of how they act when positive things happen to you. Do you pick up a weird vibe or hint of jealousy as if your success or good fortune is a commentary on their perceived shortcoming? Do they throw small jabs disguised as humor but it's really an insult intended to level you?

Anyone who tries to level you has you on a pedestal and they want you to come down. It's like your success is somehow a negative reflection of them. This couldn't be further from the truth. They have a Jane within that they need to part ways with and you need to say goodbye to this so-called friend.

What can you do to break up with Jane Type 3?

Dear Jane

_____

_____

_____

_____

_____

_____

_____

Jane Type 4—Dem Religious Folk

I grew up in the church and many religious folk are Janes. Some of them judge, condemn, shame and scrutinize you. Instead of being a safe place where people can come as they are and leave better than when they came, it's a place where you go in sick and come out sicker. Not good. Anything that is meant for your good is good—not evil, rejecting, demoralizing. Hazing of any kind, shame and guilt is never a form of love. If you are hearing you're not holy enough, pure enough, saved enough, giving enough, you might want to write the Dear Jane letter as soon as possible.

What can you do to break up with Jane Type 4?

Dear Jane

_____

_____

_____

_____

_____

_____

_____

_____

_____

Jane Type 5—Your Partner

Does your partner try to dim your shine, embarrass you, shame and ridicule you? Does your partner unfairly compare you to others, trying to make you feel less? Are they not accepting of and supportive of all of you? Are they jealous, putting you down, abusive verbally or physically? Do they try to talk you out of achieving your dreams, expanding and growing? Run chile!

What can you do to break up with Jane Type 5?

Dear Jane

_____

_____

_____

_____

_____

_____

_____

_____

These descriptions represent just a few Jane types. You might be able to identify more. What are the Janes in your life that you need to have a heart-to-heart with and make a decision to let go?

Now choose just one Jane that you will let go. Who or what is it? What will be your first step?

After you complete your Dear Jane letter, dedicate time to writing your Hello John letter—Joy and Opportunity is Happening Now! You've done the hard work. You have gone through the process of releasing, regrouping, redirecting, recovering, rebuilding, and remembering.

Congratulations! You have rid yourself of the faulty and limiting belief that something is wrong with you only to discover that the real culprit is the Jane that resides around and in you. Jane is just additional negative energy that you don't need and don't want.

It's time to say, "Hello John." I've started the first sentence for you. Now you can complete it.

Hello John, I am so grateful for the joy and opportunity that is happening to me right now . . .

_____

_____

_____

_____

_____

_____

_____

_____

_____

_____

_____

_____

Chapter 7:

Reflect

Reflect/ri-flekt/
Verb

"Think deeply or carefully about."
—*Oxford Languages*

Reflect

One day I was sitting, thinking about why I was experiencing certain unpleasant things at work. In a moment of depression and frustration of my experience with a real live person I will call Jane I penned this poem. I'm not sure about all that had happened that day or all I was feeling at the time.

I can't recall if there was a specific incident that prompted this writing or if it was a culmination of a series of events that forced a release. Honestly, I don't even remember writing it until I found it in my notes. I mean I vaguely remember writing it from a place of pain yet undeniable strength, resiliency and determination. I was in a trance. I was not fully conscious. I can't explain it.

Take what you will from this writing. Each time I read it, depending on the day and mood, it has a different meaning. Some days the cloud of whiteness represents confusion, fog, inability to see, smoking mirrors. Some days it reflects the racism that still exists in this world and its impact on me. It reflects my rebirth, my awakening, my courage and willingness to call a thing a thing. Take what you will from this writing. My hope is that it causes you to reflect and to *think deeply and carefully about all that you've read in this book. Blessings.*

• • • • • • • • • • • • • • • • • • • •

I thought it was my blackness—but realized it wasn't my blackness after all that was the cause of my dark experiences. For my blackness is what makes me confident, strong, enduring. Versatile, classic and always in fashion, like the little black dress.

A social awakening has occurred. I see the light. I've been shrouded in a cloud of whiteness. Whiteness surrounded me, hanging on, weighing me down, wrapping me thickly and tightly like a polar bear hug intended to suffocate not to infuse love, choking me until I manage to mutter—I can't breathe. Struggling to break free.

Free to use my beautiful voice, uniquely mine and divine. To cut through the cloud of whiteness, blinding and yielding meant to stop me in my tracks, keep me in place or moving slowly and cautiously—like one would wading through heavy dangerous fog.

It's an illusion, a trick, a game. The game of obscure rules, setting me up to lose. The game that requires me to rise to a higher standard to live by your double standard. It's a win-lose proposition. You continue to win and when I am close to winning, the rules change to ensure loss.

I get it, unlike the little black dress that is strong and versatile, always in fashion, the white frock is going out of fashion. What will you do? The world is turning inside out. The perpetual white party is over. You now fear finding yourself in a cloud of blackness.

But *not to worry. Unlike the cloud of whiteness meant to skew vision, the cloud of blackness embraces, comforts, accepts, loves. It's a place of rest—everyone can breathe deeply and exhale.*

I won't be afraid, I will be determined. This is my destiny, to use my breath to blow away the cloud of whiteness that binds and blinds.

● ● ● ● ● ● ● ● ● ● ● ● ● ● ● ● ● ● ●

Endnotes

[1] Parmeet Singh Sood, "Seven Things That Affect Your Vibrational Frequency from the Point of View of Quantum Physics," LinkedIn, February 20, 2019. https://www.linkedin.com/pulse/7-things-affect-your-vibrational-frequency-from-point-sood/

[2] Michael Martinez, "For Sale: Teenage Love (or Not) Letters by Jackie Kennedy Onassis," CNN.com, April 22, 2011. http://www.cnn.com/2011/SHOWBIZ/celebrity.news.gossip/04/22/auction.letters.jackie.kennedy/index.html

[3] Jamie Ducharme, "How to Tell If You're in a Toxic Relationship—And What to Do about It," TIME, June 5, 2018. https://time.com/5274206/toxic-relationship-signs-help/

[4] Songwriter: Don Schlitz, "The Gambler" lyrics, copyright Sony/ATV Music Publishing, 1976.

[5] "Pride Goes before a Fall," English for Students. https://www.english-for-students.com/pride-goes-before-a-fall.html

[6] Songwriters: Andre Young / Bernard Worrell / Charles C. Carter / Clarence Satchell / David C. Weldon / David Spradley / Eric Wright / Gary Shider / George Clinton / Gregory Webster / Le Roy Roosevelt Bonner / Lorenzo Patterson / Marshall Jones / Marvin Pierce / Norman Napier / Oshea Jackson / Ralph Middlebrooks / Roger Parker / Steven R. Arrington / Walter Morrison / Waung Hankerson / William De Vaughn / William Earl Collins. "It's On" lyrics, copyright Avery L Johnson dba Stonewater Music Publishing, BMG Rights Management, DistroKid, 1993.

[7] Songwriters: Daniel A. Johnson / Ester Dean / Jeremy Michael Coleman / Onika Tanya Maraj / Roahn Kirk Hylton. "Super Bass" lyrics, copyright Kobalt Music Publishing Ltd., Peermusic Publishing, Songtrust Ave., Sony/ATV Music Publishing LLC, Universal Music Publishing Group, Warner Chappell Music, Inc., 2010.

[8] Songwriters: Charlie Peacock / John White / Joy Elizabeth Williams. "The One That Got Away" lyrics, copyright BMG Rights Management, Spirit Music Group, Twenty Ten Music, 2013.

[9] Robert T. Kiyosaki and Sharon Lechter, Rich Dad Poor Dad: What the Rich Teach Their Kids about Money That the Poor and Middle Class Do Not! 1997.

[10] Songwriters: Ina Wroldsen / James Arthur / Tiago Miguel Amaral Carvalho. "Recovery" lyrics, copyright Reverb Music, Music Of Liberal Arts Publishing, Songs Of Universal Inc., 2013.

[11] Songwriters: Christopher Brian Bridges, Leonardo V. Mollings, Faheem Rasheed Najm, William Leonard Roberts, Johnny David Mollings, Cordazar Calvin Jr. Broadus, Khaled Mohammed Khaled. "All I Do Is Win" lyrics copyright Universal Music

Publishing Group, Sony/ATV Music Publishing LLC, Kobalt Music Publishing Ltd., 2010.

[12] Quote Investigator. "Will Rogers popularized the statement attributed to him in the 1935 movie [*Life Begins at* 40]. QI believes that he also created it. Over time the statement was replicated and modified. The year sequence was changed from 20, 30, 40 to 20, 40, 60. Also, the viewpoint presented in the first two parts was swapped. These changes generated the modern version. Thus, the modern saying does not have a single author." https://quoteinvestigator.com/2019/06/01/worry/

[13] Sarah Prout, "Ten Ways Prosperity Mindsets Think Differently," February 27, 2017. https://sarahprout.com/prosperity-mindset/

[14] Divorce Statistics: Over 115 Studies, Facts and Rates for 2022." https://www.wf-lawyers.com/divorce-statistics-and-facts/

[15] Darren Hardy, *The Compound Effect: Jumpstart Your Income, Your Life, Your Success*. 2021.

[16] Jamie Glenn, *Walk Tall, You're a Daughter of God*, 1994.

About the Author

L ori Gentles is a high-energy self-starter on a mission to help great people become greater. A radical believer in the power of intelligent, intentional, inspired, individual choice (#iChoice), she parlayed her years of experience as a human resources leader to start The Choices Company.

Her flagship program, Employee-ship, The Path to Leadership, is a refreshing departure from the conventional and reinforces total personal responsibility instead of entitlement. Her message of iChoice and her commitment to helping highly self-motivated individuals pursue possibilities without limitation has garnered the praise of peers and business leaders. "What you own, you can change" is her motto.

Her debut book, Oh SLAP! My Choices Determine My Destiny – The #1 Guide to Making Better Decisions and Living a Self-Empowered Life, solidified her place in the leadership and personal development genre. Dear Jane, It's Not Me… Saying Goodbye to Self-Criticism and Hello to Self-Love, Courage, and Confidence leaves no doubt that she was born to inspire.

More on Lori Gentles

For more information about Lori, visit
www.thechoicescompany.com.

Connect with and follow Lori and the tribe of like-minded, self-motivated achievers on instagram @weareichoice.

To have Lori Gentles speak to your organization about the principles found in Dear Jane or Oh Slap! or other self-leadership insights, visit www.thechoicescompany.com.

www.ingramcontent.com/pod-product-compliance
Lightning Source LLC
Chambersburg PA
CBHW070126030426
42335CB00016B/2279